Thinking Like a
SCIENTIST

THINKING LIKE A SCIENTIST

GRADE 5

Lessons That Develop Habits of Mind and Thinking Skills for Young Scientists

LENORE TEEVAN

William & Mary
School of Education

CENTER FOR GIFTED EDUCATION

P.O. Box 8795
Williamsburg, VA 23187

Edited by Stephanie McCauley

Cover design and layout design by Micah Benson

ISBN-13: 978-1-61821-826-1

Prufrock Press Inc.
P.O. Box 8813
Waco, TX 76714-8813
Phone: (800) 998-2208
Fax: (800) 240-0333
http://www.prufrock.com

TABLE OF CONTENTS

INTRODUCTION

PURPOSE

For the grade 5 science teacher, there is a wealth of science content to teach. How teachers approach this content to best convey it to students is key. Teachers should employ strategies that encourage students to explore content like scientists. For high-achieving students, the need to interact with and investigate ideas is central.

The purpose of this book is to provide you with lessons and strategies to engage students and help them achieve their potential. Although the examples in this book align with the Next Generation Science Standards (NGSS) for grade 5, they can also be made more rigorous for higher grade levels. It is my goal to help you reach your students by extending the lessons and inspiring your students to learn more.

ORGANIZATION OF THE BOOK

Thinking Like a Scientist is designed to guide students to understand how scientists approach problems, investigations, and research. Unit 1 introduces students to types of scientists and what scientists' work entails. The lessons in this unit will engage students as they delve into scientific career possibilities. Students will use literacy skills as they read, summarize, and paraphrase information about the work of scientists. By learning more about scientists, students may also be able to imagine themselves as scientists.

Unit 2 focuses on the scientific method. Students will use their skills of making observations and inferences as they form hypotheses. They will also employ critical thinking skills as they evaluate data and visual representations of data, such as charts and graphs.

Unit 3 explores the roles of questioning claims, evaluating evidence, and assessing experimentation, as well as the changing nature of science. Students will learn that they can uncover and correct misconceptions through experimentation and evidence. The self-correcting nature of science is upheld by the practice of testing hypotheses and gathering data. Students will engage in activities to investigate misconceptions and analyze claims.

Unit 4 covers critical thinking skills used in science. Students will apply these skills by questioning what data represent and uncovering the claims, evidence, and reasoning in scientific articles and texts. Model-making also requires the creativity and critical thinking skills of scientists. Students will be tasked with making models of natural phenomena and explaining the reasoning behind the formulation of these models.

Unit 5 includes several projects that involve the skills students have learned in the preceding units. Through practicing the thinking skills of scientists, students will perform the roles of scientists as they observe, make inferences, develop hypotheses, experiment, and communicate scientific findings. In the culminating project, students will work as part of a team to conduct research and experiments. Teachers can extend these activities by working with students to develop a project involving the school or the community.

Thinking Like a Scientist also includes a pre- and postassessment to be completed before and after the units.

SCIENCE NOTEBOOKS

A simple composition notebook, supplied by the teacher, can lend itself to a world of possibilities when it is used as a science notebook. This notebook contains students' record-keeping of their scientific learning. Organized and personalized, it has certain features to help students arrange science content coherently and meaningfully. It should contain a Table of Contents, page numbers, and dates and subjects for each entry. Students should write in their notebooks daily as they take notes, respond to prompts, and record data. Additionally, students can use graphic organizers to better understand content.

At the end of each lesson, you may want to provide a prompt for students to reflect on the lesson. Many lessons in this book contain reflection prompts in the Extension Activities sections. Students will write several sentences about what they have learned and the questions they may have. These entries communicate students' depth of understanding and any misconceptions they may have. Teacher feedback should occur at frequent intervals and be specific to student writing (e.g., "Can you tell me more about the effects of erosion, especially on mountains?" or "How do you know that this effect is a result of erosion?").

These science notebooks are not just a tool for formative assessment; they are prized and treasured repositories of student artifacts. Students may keep leaves from a field trip inside their notebooks. They might also design creative covers using designer tape, drawings, photos, and stickers. More ideas on creating and using science notebooks can be found online at https://www.fossweb.com/delegate/ssi-wdf-ucm-webContent?dDocName=D1423685.

STANDARDS

The lessons in this book align with the Next Generation Science Standards. You can find more information about the standards used in each unit in the Next Generation Science Standards Alignment and the Common Core State Standards Alignment sections of the book.

PROFESSIONAL DEVELOPMENT AND CONTINUING EDUCATION

By participating in science education, such as research or a graduate science course, you can model real-world science applications to your students. A multitude of research opportunities and professional development programs provide insight and the ability to actively participate in science. The following are a few in which I have participated and highly recommend.

- **The Maury Project:** This 2-week summer professional development held at the U.S. Naval Academy is for K–12 teachers who want to learn physical oceanography. For more information, visit https://www.ametsoc.org/ams/index.cfm/education-careers/education-program/k-12-teachers/maury-project.

- **American Wilderness Leadership School:** This is an 8-day summer professional development workshop held near Jackson, WY. This professional development may be especially useful when teaching about land use issues. For more information, visit https://safariclubfoundation.org/american-wilderness-leadership-school.

- **Chesapeake Bay Foundation Professional Learning:** There is an assortment of 5-day summer immersion programs involving hands-on research pertaining to the Chesapeake Bay. For more information, visit http://www.cbf.org/join-us/education-program/professional-learning.

- **PolarTREC (Teachers and Researchers Exploring and Collaborating):** In this program, teachers from the United States spend 3–6 weeks participating in hands-on field research experiences in the polar regions. The goal is to invigorate polar science education and understanding by bringing educators and polar researchers together. For more information, visit https://www.polartrec.com.

- **Biological Sciences Curriculum Study (BSCS) Digging Deeper:** BSCS provides professional development and lessons on plants, as well as scientist mentoring opportunities. Teacher participants can facilitate online communication and mentor student scientists as they design and carry out their own experiments. For more information, visit https://bscs.org/digging-deeper-information.

- **National Endowment for the Humanities Summer Programs:** Although these programs are humanities-oriented, some may be useful for making crosscurricular connections. For example, *The Power of Place: Land and Peoples of Appalachia* allowed teachers to integrate the geology of the Appalachian Mountains with the literature of this region. For more information, visit https://www.neh.gov/divisions/education/summer-programs.

- **National Oceanic and Atmospheric Administration (NOAA) Teacher at Sea:** Science teachers can apply to work aboard a research ship. For more information, visit https://teacheratsea.noaa.gov/#/about/cruises.

With some of these professional development activities, it is possible for students to be engaged while the teacher is in the field. For example, PolarTREC holds PolarConnect events, which allow students to learn about the research while the teacher is participating as a scientist in the field. In addition, students are able to correspond with their teacher during PolarTREC and NOAA Teacher at Sea expeditions by reading their teacher's daily blogs about the work of scientists and asking questions online. This interaction with their teachers, scientists, and crew members engages students and opens up possible avenues of exploration.

THINKING LIKE SERIES

This book is one in a series, developed in conjunction with the Center for Gifted Education at William & Mary, intended to develop process skills in various content areas and enhance discipline-specific thinking and habits of mind through hands-on activities. Each book in the series focuses on a specific discipline and grade level:

- In *Thinking Like a Geographer*, students in grade 2 develop and practice geography skills, such as reading and creating maps, graphs, and charts; examine primary and secondary sources; and think spatially on a variety of scales.
- In *Thinking Like a Mathematician*, students in grade 3 engage in exploration activities, complete mathematical challenges, and then apply what they have learned by making real-world connections.
- In *Thinking Like an Engineer*, students in grade 4 complete design challenges, visit with an engineer, and investigate real-world problems to plan feasible engineering solutions.
- In *Thinking Like a Scientist*, students in grade 5 use inquiry-based investigations to explore what scientists do, engage in critical thinking, learn about scientific tools and research, and examine careers in scientific fields.

PREASSESSMENT

The preassessment will help you establish a baseline of what your students know about experimental variables and design. Ideally, this assessment should be administered at the beginning of the year or sometime before the final unit so that you can make sure that students understand the parts of an experiment.

The preassessment includes an experimental scenario for students to analyze. Although these are multiple-choice questions, they can easily be made into open-ended questions. Open-ended questions require students to craft their own explanations, and students' responses are often more insightful than responses to multiple-choice items. Depending on the type of data you need from your students, you can assess your students either way.

When evaluating student performance on the preassessment, identify the most frequently missed questions so that you can clarify any misconceptions and reinforce the material by incorporating it into other lessons. For example, students frequently confuse "independent" and "dependent" variables. Perhaps you will be teaching the parts of an experiment in a later lesson. However, you can reinforce the meanings and uses of these terms in lessons taught prior to that of experimental design.

PREASSESSMENT

Directions: Please read the paragraph below and answer the questions that follow.

Jan is working on her science fair project on types of soil fertilizers. She has four large pots with 100 bean seeds in each. In Pot A, she adds Fertilizer A. She adds Fertilizer B to Pot B, and Fertilizer C to Pot C. In the last pot, she does not add any fertilizer. She makes sure each pot is watered with the same amount of water at the same time. All pots have the same amount of sunlight and the same air temperature. After 2 months, Jan will measure the height of the plants.

1. What is the independent variable?
   a. The amount of water
   b. The amount of sunlight
   c. The types of soil fertilizer
   d. The height of the plants

2. What is the dependent variable?
   a. The amount of water
   b. The amount of sunlight
   c. The types of soil fertilizer
   d. The height of the plants

3. What are the constants?
   a. The amount of water, the amount of sunlight, and the bean seeds
   b. The amount of sunlight and types of fertilizers
   c. The air temperature and the seeds without fertilizer
   d. The different watering times and the air temperatures

4. What is the control in this experiment?
   a. The pot with Fertilizer A
   b. The pot with no fertilizer
   c. The pot with Fertilizer B
   d. The pot with Fertilizer C

Preassessment, continued

5. Why is it important to have a control in this experiment?
    a. Plant growth with and without fertilizers can be compared.
    b. The effect of watering the plants can be measured.
    c. The effects of sunlight and water on plant growth can be studied.
    d. The bean seeds will not grow without a control.

6. To which branch of science does Jan's science experiment most closely relate?
    a. Earth Science
    b. Chemistry
    c. Botany
    d. Oceanography

7. On what will Jan base her conclusions?
    a. The books she read
    b. The data collected from her experiment
    c. Her impressions and opinions of the experiment
    d. The information she learned about plants in class

8. What are some possible variables that might interfere with her findings?
    a. Insects might eat plants in the pot farther away from others.
    b. The changing seasons might affect the plant growth.
    c. There might be a few days of rainy weather.
    d. The bean seeds might be affected by the fertilizers.

9. How should Jan represent her findings?
    a. Pie chart
    b. Bar graph
    c. Drawings
    d. Table

10. When Jan has completed the science fair, what might her next step(s) be?
    a. Communicate her results to the school garden committee
    b. Redesign her experiment using another type of seed
    c. Repeat her experiment to see if she has the same results
    d. All of the above

UNIT 1
WHAT DO SCIENTISTS DO?

RATIONALE

Donning goggles and lab coats, students feel like scientists when they engage in the skills of making observations, collecting data, and drawing conclusions. By actively participating in scientific inquiry in class, students glimpse what it is like to be a scientist. High-achieving students will want to know more about scientific careers and the types of scientists and research. They can gauge the appeal of various careers by researching those of interest. The following lesson plans provide a platform for students to investigate and teach others about careers in science.

PLAN

In Lesson 1.1, students will describe scientists and their work through illustration and literacy. In Lesson 1.2, students will list characteristics of scientists by using a Frayer model. In addition, they will synthesize information from a text and class discussion to add to the Frayer model. In Lesson 1.3, students will build upon the previous lessons to produce a research project about careers in science.

LESSON 1.1

WHAT DOES A SCIENTIST LOOK LIKE?

RESOURCES AND MATERIALS

- Lesson 1.1 Draw-a-Scientist Test

ESTIMATED TIME

50 minutes

OBJECTIVES

In this lesson, students will:
- illustrate their conceptions of a scientist, and
- explain their illustrations through reflection.

CONTENT

The Draw-a-Scientist Test (DAST; Chambers, 1983) was developed as a means of assessing stereotypes regarding scientists. This informal test is simple to administer but reveals important conceptions that students hold about what a scientist looks like and does as a career.

PRIOR KNOWLEDGE

Students should have learned about some different types of scientists from school, home, and popular culture. For example, children may have parents or friends whose parents are scientists. Additionally, many children are aware of the stereotypical "mad scientist" from cartoons and movies.

INSTRUCTIONAL SEQUENCE

1. Distribute Lesson 1.1 Draw-a-Scientist Test and instruct students to draw a scientist. You may specify to students that their scientists should be "doing science." Allow students no more that 15 minutes to complete the task.
2. When students have completed the handout, they can display their products and compare them to other students' drawings.
3. Ask students: *What do you notice about the drawings? How are they similar? How are they different?* Students can discuss in small groups or with partners, and then share their impressions with the class.
4. Have students use what they learned from the DAST as a springboard to think about themselves as scientists. Questions to ask include:
   - What is your scientist doing? What do you like to do while doing science?
   - What might a scientist find difficult to do? What is difficult for you to do while you are doing science?
   - Most students drew White men as their scientists. Can anyone be a scientist? Why is it important to have scientists from diverse backgrounds? What can we learn from each other?

EXTENSION ACTIVITIES

- Have students write a reflection paragraph about this activity. They may respond to the following questions:
  - Can you imagine yourself as a scientist?
  - What type of scientist would you like to be?
  - What types of science activities do you like doing?

- If you administer the DAST at the beginning of the year, keep these drawings until the end of the school year. By then, students should have been exposed to female and male scientists of diverse backgrounds. Administer the DAST a second time at the end of the year and have students compare their earlier drawings to their most recent ones. Follow-up questions can probe how and why the drawings are different (e.g., *What do you understand now about scientists that you didn't understand at the beginning of the year?*).

ASSESSMENT OBSERVATIONS

- Students should draw scientists who are reflective of the students.
- Students should draw their scientist engaging in scientific activities, such as using scientific tools and measurements. (*Note.* A rating scale for the DAST is available online, if quantitative data are needed. The rating scale evaluates gender, symbols of typical scientists, attire, research, and technology.)

LESSON 1.1

Draw-a-Scientist Test

Directions: In the space below, draw a picture of a scientist doing science.

Draw-a-Scientist Test, continued

1. Describe what this scientist is doing.

2. List three adjectives that describe this scientist.

LESSON 1.2

WHAT IS A SCIENTIST?

RESOURCES AND MATERIALS

- Lesson 1.2 Frayer Model
- Class Frayer model (projected or drawn on the board)
- Web resources:
  - "What Is Science and Who Are Scientists?" by National Institute of Environmental Health Sciences (https://kids.niehs.nih.gov/topics/how-science-works/science-scientists/index.htm)
  - "STEM Career Kids" by McGraw-Hill Education (https://www.mheducation.com/prek-12/program/microsites/MKTSP-AIB01M0/stem-career-kids.html)

ESTIMATED TIME

30 minutes

OBJECTIVE

In this lesson, students will define "scientist" by completing a Frayer model.

CONTENT

The Frayer model is a means by which students can build upon preexisting knowledge and fit new content into a framework. This tool helps students retain new knowledge and think more critically about content as they are interacting with the denotation and characteristics of a topic.

PRIOR KNOWLEDGE

Students should have some background knowledge of scientists and what scientists do, gathered from school and popular culture. They may have seen science programs on television or at school featuring scientists, such as paleontologists or meteorologists.

INSTRUCTIONAL SEQUENCE

1. Divide students into small groups of 2–3. Instruct students to discuss examples of scientists. These scientists can be ones that students know or have seen in popular media.
2. Distribute Lesson 1.2 Frayer Model for students to complete individually. Review the parts of the Frayer model if necessary. Students will need to generate a definition, characteristics, examples, and nonexamples of "scientist."
3. After 5 minutes, have students return to their groups and discuss their definitions and examples with group members. Students may add information to their Frayer model if necessary.
4. Ask each group to choose a spokesperson to share the group's ideas with the rest of the class. Each spokesperson should present his or her group's findings.
5. As the spokespersons present, have a student (or students) write the examples on a class Frayer model and arrange them in relevant groups. For example, students might group the types of scientists in the biological sciences together. During the class discussion, students may also give examples of nonscientists. For example, a student might contribute "astrologist" and "hypnotist," which should be placed in the nonexample quadrant.
6. Provide students with a short reading on types of scientists (see Resources and Materials or your adopted science textbook). When they have finished reading, have students work with partners to enter more words and ideas into each of the Frayer model quadrants.

EXTENSION ACTIVITY

Have students keep track of the types of scientists they learn about in their science notebooks. They should start a list and add to it each time they learn of a new type of scientist. You might also create a board in the classroom with the heading "Types of Scientists," to which students can add throughout the year.

ASSESSMENT OBSERVATION

Students should have completed a meaningful Frayer model with a definition of "scientist."

LESSON 1.2
Frayer Model

Directions: Complete the Frayer model for the the word "scientist." Define the word and give characteristics, examples, and nonexamples of a scientist.

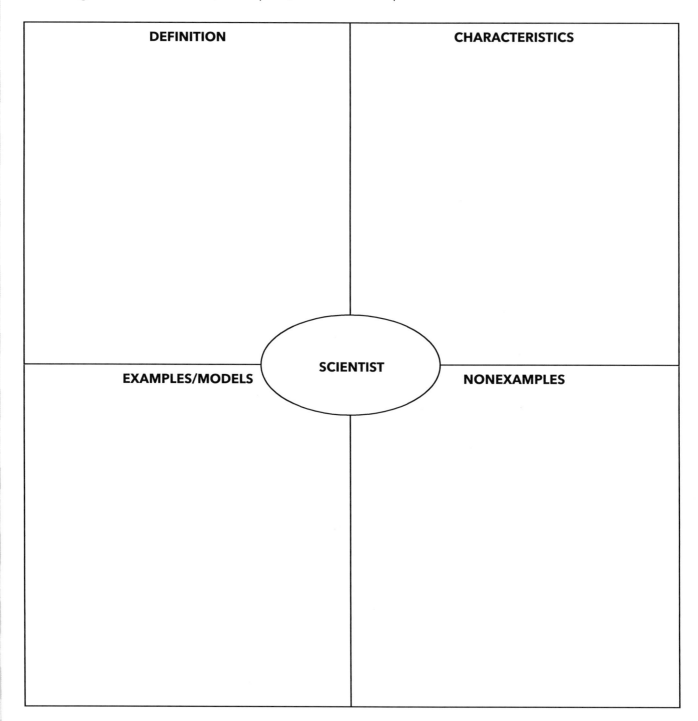

LESSON 1.3

PROJECT: SCIENTIFIC CAREERS

RESOURCES AND MATERIALS

- Lesson 1.3 Explore a Career in Science
- Lesson 1.3 Scientist Interview Questions
- Lesson 1.3 Rubric
- Materials for posters (e.g., posters, paper, markers, etc.)
- Sticky notes

ESTIMATED TIME

Three class periods to prepare information, conduct scientist interviews, and complete the gallery walk

OBJECTIVES

In this lesson, students will:
- organize and discuss information related to a scientific career of interest,
- display what they have learned in a gallery walk, and
- respond to other students' displays during the gallery walk.

CONTENT

Students will have the opportunity to explore and investigate science careers of interest. They will also receive feedback from peers and teachers so that they can further their exploration of a scientific career.

PRIOR KNOWLEDGE

Students should know some specific types of scientists. Students probably have a favorite topic in science and may know about scientists in that area of science. In addition, they may personally know scientists.

INSTRUCTIONAL SEQUENCE

1. Introduce the research assignment to students. Each student will choose a type of scientist to research and answer questions to guide his or her exploration. Distribute Lesson 1.3 Explore a Career in Science and set a deadline for the research.

2. Tell students that they will be interviewing scientists as part of their projects. There are several ways to find scientists for students to interview. If there is a university nearby, you might invite scientists to give short presentations about their scientific careers. You might also contact the school's Parent Teacher Association and ask parent scientists to visit the classroom to talk about their careers. Skype a Scientist (https://www.skypeascientist. com) is another way for students to hear from scientists in the field or lab in real time.

3. Distribute Lesson 1.3 Scientist Interview Questions to guide students as they plan and conduct their interviews. Students should add three additional questions that are relevant to their specific scientists.

4. Explain that students will compile the information they learn and organize it on a poster to be used in a Career Gallery Walk. Each poster should include the following information (see Lesson 1.3 Explore a Career in Science).
   - The type of scientist
   - The scientist's field of study
   - The education and experience needed to become this type of scientist
   - A typical day in the career of this scientist
   - Prospects for scientists in this field 10–15 years from now
   - Important aspects of the scientific career that students learned from doing this project
   - Images of the scientist "doing science" and the tools of this type of science

5. Provide students with Lesson 1.3 Rubric for the project. Ask students questions about the rubric, such as "What kind of project/presentation would receive a 4?"

6. Allow time for students to research, interview their scientists, and create their posters.

7. Conduct the gallery walk. Students can display their posters around the room or in the hallway and then examine the posters of the other students. (*Note.* You might also accept a student-made video as an alternative to a

poster. In this case, accommodations should be made to project the video during the gallery walk.)

8. Have students write comments on sticky notes about other students' projects. Direct students to focus on what they learned from the displays of others. For example, a student might leave a note saying, "I never knew that doctors could specialize in face transplants. I'd like to learn more about that." Additionally, students can also comment on how others organized their displays (e.g., "Your video showed the lab technician using the micropipettes, and then you began interviewing the scientist. This made me want to find out more about laboratory work."). The skills gained by evaluating research products can help students improve their research projects in the future.

EXTENSION ACTIVITIES

- Have students reflect on one or more of the following prompts in their science notebooks:
  - What have you learned from this research project?
  - What would you like to learn more about?
  - Which scientific career is most appealing to you? How can you work to develop the skills needed for this career?

- If applicable, guide students toward other resources that might interest them, or connect them with a scientist mentor.

ASSESSMENT OBSERVATIONS

- Students should be active participants in all components of the project.
- Students' visual displays should be complete and creative.

LESSON 1.3

Explore a Career in Science

Directions: Complete this form to help you choose a type of scientist to research. Ask your teacher to approve your answers before you begin the project.

1. What type of scientist are you interested in learning more about?

2. In which area of science does this type of scientist work?

3. Where does this type of scientist work?

4. What is a typical workday like for this type of scientist?

5. What interests you the most about this career?

6. What interests you the least about this career?

Thinking Like a Scientist © Prufrock Press Inc.

Explore a Career in Science, continued

7. What will this career look like in the future?

8. What kind of education and job experience do you need for this career?

9. To whom can you speak to learn more about this career?

10. What other question(s) do you have about this career?

Scientific Career Project

Create a poster to share the research you have compiled about your type of scientist. Your poster should include the following information:
1. The type of scientist
2. This scientist's field of study
3. The education and experience needed to become this type of scientist
4. A typical day in the career of this scientist
5. Prospects for scientists in this field 10–15 years from now
6. Important aspects of this scientific career that you learned from completing the project
7. Images of the scientist doing science and the tools of this type of science

LESSON 1.3
Scientist Interview Questions

Directions: Use the following interview questions to guide your meeting with a scientist. Consider your scientist's particular field, place of work, or interests.

1. What type of scientist are you?

2. What is a typical day at work like for you?

3. What do you like most about being a scientist?

4. What do you like least about being a scientist?

5. How did you decide to become a scientist?

Scientist Interview Questions, continued

6. What kind of education should someone in your field have?

7. What are some interesting topics to learn about in your field?

8. _____?

9. _____?

10. _____?

LESSON 1.3
Rubric

	4	3	2	1
Information	The student's finished product shows evidence of all of the resources. The facts are presented coherently in the final product.	The student's finished product shows evidence of most of the resources. The facts are presented mostly coherently in the final product.	The student's finished product shows evidence of some of the resources. The facts are presented somewhat coherently in the final product.	The student's finished product shows evidence of none of the resources. The facts are not presented coherently in the final product.
Research	The student restated the research done for this project in his or her own words. The synthesized information shows great depth of understanding.	The student restated the research done for this project mostly in his or her own words. The synthesized information shows a very good understanding.	The student restated the research done for this project somewhat in his or her own words. The synthesized information shows a good understanding.	The student did not restate the research done for this project in his or her own words. The synthesized information shows little understanding.
Mechanics	There are no grammatical and/or punctuation errors. The writing style flows very well.	There are few grammatical and/or punctuation errors. The writing style flows well.	There are some grammatical and/or punctuation errors. The writing style is sometimes halting.	There are many grammatical and/or punctuation errors. The writing style is very halting.

UNIT 2
WHAT IS THE SCIENTIFIC METHOD?

RATIONALE

Science is a way of knowing and understanding natural phenomena through investigation and exploration. All branches of science, such as astronomy, biology, chemistry, physics, and geology, adhere to the objective means of understanding natural events. In their everyday lives, students also follow the scientific method, although not as stringently as a scientist would. Students might employ this approach as they try to repair a broken computer or construct an innovative machine. In all cases, what drives high-achieving students to investigate is a desire to know and understand.

When students realize that they use scientific processes in a multitude of situations, they not only realize the importance of this objective means of problem solving, but also incorporate critical thinking skills, such as making observations, inferences, and drawing conclusions, that underlie the scientific method. In effect, they are thinking like scientists in their daily lives.

PLAN

In Lesson 2.1, students will employ the scientific skills of observation and making inferences to draw conclusions. In Lesson 2.2, students will evaluate hypotheses and determine testable predictions. In Lesson 2.3, students will evaluate data so that they can draw strong conclusions. In Lesson 2.4, students will evaluate graphs and charts and decide how well they represent the data. In Lesson 2.5, students will incorporate the scientific skills of devising hypotheses and evaluating data as they carry out an inquiry-based experiment.

LESSON 2.1

OBSERVING MYSTERY OBJECTS

RESOURCES AND MATERIALS

- Lesson 2.1 Observing Mystery Objects
- Four mystery objects that can be handled by students (e.g., ping-pong ball, seeds, cotton balls, small bells, clay, leaves, velvet; attention should be given to any allergies students have)
- Four numbered boxes, paper sandwich bags, or dark plastic sacks to hide the mystery objects
- Web resources:
  - "Biographies for Kids: Scientists and Inventors" by Ducksters (https://www.ducksters.com/biography/scientists/scientists_and_inventors.php)
  - "Featured Authors/Scientists" by Buffalo and Erie County Public Library (https://www.buffalolib.org/content/milestones-science/featured-authors-scientists)
  - "Podcast Partners" by The Walking Classroom (https://www.thewalkingclassroom.org/our-program/podcast-partners)

ESTIMATED TIME

1 hour

OBJECTIVES

In this lesson, students will:
- use the skills of observation and making inferences to draw conclusions, and
- relate this activity to the nature of science, using examples.

CONTENT

There are several ways to set up an inquiry in the classroom. An inquiry might begin with a question or a situation for which students must explore possible answers. To model this type of inquiry, engage students by presenting them with containers that hold mystery contents. Students will employ their senses to make observations and then draw upon their observations to make inferences.

PRIOR KNOWLEDGE

Students should have experience with identifying a range of textures.

INSTRUCTIONAL SEQUENCE

1. Present students with a set of numbered boxes (or bags), each with a mystery item inside. Instruct students to either shake the boxes in which the items are placed or physically handle the items within the bag without looking.
2. Using Lesson 2.1 Observing Mystery Objects, have students supply adjectives for each object and, based on their observations, make an inference about what each object is.
3. When students have completed their inferences, reveal what each box contains. Discuss with the class which objects were hard to identify and the observations that helped students identify these objects. Students should give evidence for their choices (e.g., "I knew it was a rubber band because I could stretch it, and it snapped back!").
4. Explain that the observational and critical thinking skills that students used to identify the objects are what scientists use: *The seeds of scientific investigation come from observations. The science content we learn now was discovered through the observations of scientists. In the case of plate tectonics, for example, scientists observed similar fossils and rock types on different continents and asked questions. Finding answers to those questions entailed following the scientific method. Science is a means of "finding out."*
5. Relate the experiment to students' everyday lives by asking for specific examples of how students relied on observations as part of their problem-solving procedure. This activity can be referred to throughout the year as students complete labs and projects that require observations and inferences.

EXTENSION ACTIVITIES

- Have students read short biographies of scientists (see Resources and Materials), noting how the scientists used skills such as observation and inference.

- Ask students to reflect on the following in their science notebooks: *Think of a time when you made an inference based on incomplete data. Explain the experience.*

ASSIGNMENT OBSERVATIONS

- Students should use evidence to support their inferences regarding the identification of the mystery objects.
- Students may use a variety of ways to explain their observations of the mystery objects. They might offer descriptions, such as "It's squishy," or comparisons, such as "It's as soft as a rabbit's fur."

LESSON 2.1
Observing Mystery Objects

Directions: For each mystery object, write your observations. Then, write your inferences about what you think the mystery objects are.

	My Observations	**My Inferences**
Example Object	*Light, breakable, smells good, sticky*	*I think it's an orange peel.*
Object 1		
Object 2		
Object 3		
Object 4		

LESSON 2.2

EVALUATING HYPOTHESES

RESOURCES AND MATERIALS

- Lesson 2.2 Interpreting Graphs
- Lesson 2.2 Evaluating Hypotheses

ESTIMATED TIME

30 minutes

OBJECTIVES

In this lesson, students will:
- evaluate hypotheses and decide whether they can be tested, and
- use this knowledge to write hypotheses of their own.

CONTENT

In elementary school, a hypothesis is usually formulated as "If I change the *independent variable*, then the *dependent variable* will be affected" (e.g., "If I use variegated leaves, then the rate of photosynthesis will be affected"). The independent variable is the only variable changed in an experiment. Students can remember this by "*Independent* starts with an 'I,' and 'I' change this variable." The dependent variable is always quantitative; students can remember that "*dependent* and *data* both start with 'd.'" Both variables are included in the hypothesis. A hypothesis is never simply an educated guess. Instead, it should be presented to students as a testable statement about the relationship between the independent and dependent variable. The hypothesis is testable, unbiased, and opinion-free.

PRIOR KNOWLEDGE

Students should have participated in science fairs in elementary school. They may have had some previous experience writing hypotheses.

INSTRUCTIONAL SEQUENCE

1. Distribute Lesson 2.2 Interpreting Graphs for students to complete. Students should use only what they see in the graph to make conclusions about what the experiment might have included (i.e., how does mass affect the distance a paper airplane can fly?).
2. Have a class discussion about hypotheses: *What makes a good hypothesis? How can we develop good hypotheses in experiments?* Elicit student answers.
3. Distribute Lesson 2.2 Evaluating Hypotheses for students to complete with a partner. Ask students to evaluate whether each statement could function as a hypothesis. If the hypotheses are not testable or are biased, students should rewrite them.
4. Review students' revised hypotheses in a class discussion.

EXTENSION ACTIVITY

Have students create hypotheses about current events. For example, you could mention the recent occurrence of earthquakes in a particular region of the world. Ask students if locations near plate boundaries might have more earthquakes than other regions. Task students with devising a hypothesis testing whether earthquakes occur on or near plate boundaries.

ASSESSMENT OBSERVATIONS

- Students should give evidence in support of their hypotheses.
- Students should also give evidence and/or reasons explaining why some hypotheses are not supported by data.

LESSON 2.2
Interpreting Graphs

Directions: The following graph was developed by a group of students in a science class. Consider the data and then answer the questions about the experiment the class conducted.

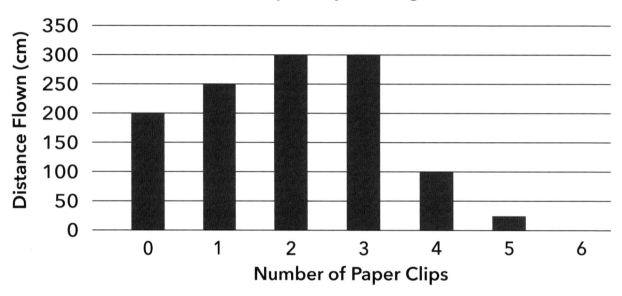

Paper Airplane Flights

1. What do you think the students were testing?

2. What do you think they predicted would happen as they added more paper clips?

Interpreting Graphs, continued

3. What do you think their hypothesis was?

4. How were they able to test this hypothesis?

5. What do you think makes a good hypothesis?

LESSON 2.2
Evaluating Hypotheses

Directions: Evaluate the hypotheses below. Rewrite any weak hypotheses in the column on the right.

Hypothesis	Is This Hypothesis Testable and Unbiased?	Revised Hypothesis
If I change the amount of salt in the recipe, the soup will taste bad.		
Blue jays prefer sunflower seeds to thistle seeds.		
The growth of plants is affected by the amount of light they receive.		
If I change the air pressure outside of the balloon, the pressure inside the balloon increases.		

LESSON 2.3

EVALUATING DATA

RESOURCES AND MATERIALS

- Lesson 2.3 Evaluating Variables
- Graph or chart paper
- Web resource for use in studying Earth's place in the universe: "Duration of Daylight/Darkness Table for One Year" (http://aa.usno.navy.mil/about/staff/docs/history.php)

ESTIMATED TIME

30 minutes

OBJECTIVES

In this lesson, students will:
- be able to distinguish discrete data from continuous data, and
- decide the best visual representation of that data.

CONTENT

Students will be provided with different types of data and will be asked to distinguish them from one another.

PRIOR KNOWLEDGE

Students should be familiar with data from previous science and math classes. In addition, they may have had to collect and display data in science fairs.

INSTRUCTIONAL SEQUENCE

1. Pose a simple question for students to respond to, such as the following: *How many of you prefer listening to music while studying?* Students can raise their hands to indicate yes.

2. Write the number of "yes" responses on the board. Ask: *How did we get these data? Did we measure anything, or did we simply count the number of students? How is that data different from measuring your height from year to year?*

3. Ask students what they notice about the two types of data. Using their observations, introduce the concepts of *discrete* and *continuous* data. As a rule, discrete data are represented in a bar graph, whereas continuous data are shown in a line graph. Discrete data are counted (e.g., the number of leaves on a plant). Continuous data are measured (e.g., height, mass, or temperature).

4. Explain to students that dependent variables are quantitative data, which must be represented visually in a graph or chart.

5. Distribute Lesson 2.3 Evaluating Variables to students in groups of 2–3. Students should evaluate the variables as either discrete or continuous and provide reasons for doing so. Each group can report its responses and reasoning.

6. In groups, have students collect data on something available in the classroom and decide how to graph the information. Examples might include student height versus arm span, the number of different types of textbooks, students' favorite animals, the temperature of the classroom throughout the day, etc.

7. Allow students time to collect and graph their data. Student groups should present their findings to the class.

EXTENSION ACTIVITIES

- Have students look for types of data in other classes and/or in the news. Students can show the class the type of data and explain why it is graphed as a bar or line graph.

- If the class is currently working on the grade 5 standards about "Earth's Place in the Universe," have students graph the day length for winter and summer solstices and the fall and spring equinoxes. The website listed in the Resources and Materials section can provide day length for a specific latitude.

ASSESSMENT OBSERVATION

Students should be able to justify why data are discrete or continuous through definition and example.

LESSON 2.3

Evaluating Variables

Directions: Consider the variables (data) in the chart below and identify each one as either "discrete" or "continuous." Be sure to explain your reasoning for your choices.

Data	Discrete or Continuous?	Reasoning
The density of a liquid as it is heated		
The number of students who use cell phones to complete classroom assignments		
The volume of a liquid before and after it is frozen		
The number of "heads" each time a coin is flipped		
The average monthly temperature in a location throughout the year		

LESSON 2.4

EVALUATING TYPES OF GRAPHS AND CHARTS

RESOURCES AND MATERIALS

- Lesson 2.4 Choosing Graph Types
- Lesson 2.4 Graphing Personal Data
- Graph paper

ESTIMATED TIME

One class period

OBJECTIVES

In this lesson, students will evaluate data and determine which type of graph is necessary to portray the data.

CONTENT

Using the correct graph to represent data is a skill that students learn and practice throughout their science education. To communicate the results of experiments, data must be organized correctly and meaningfully in a visual representation. These visual representations of data usually take the form of a bar graph, line graph, or a pie chart. Many students, however, are mystified as to which type of graph to use. Developed by Webber, Nelson, Weatherbee, Zoellick, and Schauffler (2014), the Graph Choice Chart functions like a dichotomous key to help students decide which graph to use. The choice of graph is dependent on the research question. For example, a student might ask, "How have my grades improved over this school year?" The Graph Choice Chart would guide the student to a box asking if two numeric factors are correlated and if the research question is related to change through linear time. From this chart, the student would be guided to use a line graph.

PRIOR KNOWLEDGE

Students should have learned about graphs prior to grade 5. They will have seen graphs in other classes as well as in the media.

INSTRUCTIONAL SEQUENCE

1. As a class, set up a situation to collect data, such as taking attendance or timing how long the morning announcements run each day. Ask students how to best represent that data in a graph.
2. Students should respond with ideas and explain why they chose a particular type of graph. Have the class choose the best type of graph for the data. You may then graph the data on the board or have students create graphs on graph paper.
3. Divide students in small groups of 2–3 and distribute Lesson 2.4 Choosing Graph Types. Ask students to evaluate each research question, choose a type of graph to represent that data, and explain why they chose to represent the data that way.
4. When students have completed the handout, ask a student from each group to report the group's decisions and justifications for one of the research questions. Discuss the results as a class, using the following questions:
   - What criteria do we use to determine the best type of graph?
   - Which variable is on the x-axis?
   - Which variable is on the y-axis?
   - Which units of measurement should be used?
   - How do you determine the minimum and maximum values to use on a graph?

5. Distribute Lesson 2.4 Graphing Personal Data. Have students complete the handout, using personally relevant data, such as the amount of time spent studying or how much money they spent over the week.
6. Display students' completed graphs in the classroom. These graphs can be referred to during later lessons, as needed.

EXTENSION ACTIVITY

In their science notebooks, have students create and maintain graphs that use ongoing data. For example, students could record assessment scores on a graph and discuss the trends they see in the data. The recording of data could be for the duration of a particular unit. For example, if the unit involves the needs of plants, students may use a graph to track the growth of plants under different conditions. If students are asked to record their unit test scores, this process will entail yearlong data collection, and they should be able to use the appropriate graph and interpret the trends they see.

ASSESSMENT OBSERVATIONS

- Students should be able to create graphs with titles, a labeled x-axis and y-axis, and an evenly spaced scale.
- Students should be able to justify their choices of graphs to use.

LESSON 2.4
Choosing Graph Types

Directions: Consider each research question and decide what type of graph should be used to represent the data. Make sure you provide justification for each of your choices.

Research Question	Type of Graph	Justification
How does the amount of sea ice in the Arctic change throughout the year?	*Line graph*	*The amount of sea ice is measured over a period of time.*
What proportion of recyclable waste is thrown away at our school?		
How did the average winter temperature for last year compare to the average winter temperature for this year?		
What are the ages of students in our class?		

LESSON 2.4
Graphing Personal Data

Directions: You will be using personal data, such as the time you spent studying in the last week, to create a graph. Use what you have learned about graphs to determine the best graph for your data.

1. What kind of data would you like to compile?

2. Record your data below:

3. What kind of graph will you use to represent your data? Why?

Graphing Personal Data, continued

4. Create your graph below. You may use a separate sheet of graph paper if needed.

5. In the checklist below, place a checkmark next to each component you have com-pleted. If you are missing any components, add them to your graph.

Graph title	
Labeled *x*-axis	
Labeled *y*-axis	
Units of measurement	
Evenly spaced scale	

LESSON 2.5

TRANSFORMED "FLOATING LEAF DISK" LAB

RESOURCES AND MATERIALS

- Lesson 2.5 Experiment Planning Template
- Floating Leaf Disk Lab examples (examples can be found in most grade 5 science textbooks or in the following web resources):
    - "Photosynthesis and Floating Leaf Discs" by Steve Binkley (https://www. carolina.com/teacher-resources/Interactive/photosynthesis-and-float ing-leaf-disks/tr28604.tr)
    - "Photosynthesis: Floating Leaf Discs" by Maddie Van Beek (https:// www.discoveryexpresskids.com/blog/photosynthesis-floating-leaf-discs)

- Floating Leaf Disk Lab materials:
    - Large plastic syringes
    - Baking soda
    - Water
    - Leaves
    - Hole punch
    - Dish detergent
    - Colored plastic transparencies
    - Various types of plants

- Student computers or tablets with Internet access
- Virtual labs:
    - "Virtual Labs" by McGraw-Hill Education (http://www.glencoe.com/ sites/common_assets/science/virtual_labs/LS12/LS12.html)
    - "Measuring the Rate of Photosynthesis of Elodea" by University of Reading (https://www.reading.ac.uk/virtualexperiments/ves/preload er-photosynthesis-full.html)

ESTIMATED TIME

Two 1-hour class periods; Day 1 for the "Floating Leaf Disk" lab, and Day 2 for the transformed lab

OBJECTIVES

In this lesson, students will:
- make observations and inferences about a lab demonstration,
- formulate a new experiment of their own design, and
- implement an inquiry-based investigation by experimenting.

CONTENT

The curriculum set forth by your state and district may have mandatory laboratory activities for you to implement. If these labs are predictable, high-ability students may feel as though they are simply following a cookbook recipe. The "Floating Leaf Disc" lab is a common experiment in grade 5 photosynthesis units. To extend students' thinking, model the lab on Day 1, and then task students with building their own lab or experiment on Day 2. Having students base their planned experiments on the one they have just completed fosters the notion that science is not conducted in a vacuum; it is built upon previous research and evidence.

Other options include having students sequence the procedure after it has been taken out of sequence. Students could also formulate the hypothesis in the form of a flowchart rather than use the traditional if-then statement.

PRIOR KNOWLEDGE

Students should know basic lab procedures and safety measures.

INSTRUCTIONAL SEQUENCE

1. On Day 1, have the class conduct the Floating Leaf Disk Lab.
2. On Day 2, ask students to review what was learned from the Floating Leaf Disk Lab in a class discussion. Students should refer to their notes as they participate.
3. Ask students to work in small groups of 2–3 to devise their own experiment based on the observations and inferences they made the previous day.
4. Distribute Lesson 2.5 Experiment Planning Template for students to complete as they devise their own experiments. You may direct students online to get ideas from virtual labs (see Resources and Materials).
5. If students are still undecided on what to investigate, prompt them with questions: *We used spinach leaves in the original experiment. What do you think might happen if you use another type of leaf, such as one with trichomes (plant hairs) or variegation (multicolored leaves)? We used a heat lamp in the original experiment. What do you think might happen if you use another light condition, such as colored lights, shade, or no light?*

6. When students have completed the first part of the template, approve their answers before they proceed with their experiment.

7. Once students have their template approved, they should implement their planned experiments. (See Lesson 2.2 for more information about writing testable hypotheses.)

8. Have students complete the final two sections of Lesson 2.5 Experiment Planning Template. Based on class curriculum and student needs, have students write their experiment in the form of a lab report in their science notebooks. Alternatively, students could communicate their findings by creating a poster with the components listed in the planning template.

EXTENSION ACTIVITIES

- Have students present their experiments and findings to their peers, parents, and administrators at a school science night or open house.
- If access to a plant growth cart or a school greenhouse is available, have students plan long-term experiments based on the experiments done in class.

ASSESSMENT OBSERVATIONS

- All students should be active participants in the planning and implementation of the experiment.
- Each student group should be able to devise a relevant and testable hypothesis.

LESSON 2.5

Experiment Planning Template

Directions: Complete this handout with information about your planned experiment. Make sure your teacher approves your experiment before you begin.

What do you want to test?	The effect of _____ on _____
Independent variable *What you will change*	
Dependent variable *What you will measure*	
Constants *What you will keep the same*	
Control *What will be used for comparison*	
Materials	
Procedure	
Data *What type of data will you record? How will you represent these data?*	
Analysis *How will you interpret your data?*	

Experiment Planning Template, continued

After you have completed your experiment, consider your results.

Conclusions	
Ideas for Improvement and Future Experiments	

UNIT 3
WHAT IS THE ROLE OF EVIDENCE?

RATIONALE

Science content knowledge is continually updated and added to the textbooks and standards teachers utilize. Due to technological advances and greater collaboration among diverse types of scientists, scientific knowledge is expanding. For example, science textbooks published before 1980 most likely have no mention of exoplanet discoveries. This is a testament to the vibrant nature of science: It is changeable, and scientists are forever exploring and investigating. As a result of the evidence-based, yet tentative, nature of science, scientists must always analyze claims, refute theories, and uncover misconceptions. Engaging in these scientific skills facilitates our students' development of problem-solving and critical thinking skills. Opportunities to evaluate claims, ideas, and hypotheses abound for our students (e.g., through the advertising directed at them).

PLAN

In Lesson 3.1, students will evaluate and analyze claims in advertisements and understand the connection between claims and evidence. In Lesson 3.2, students will differentiate the scientific use of the word *theory* from the everyday use of the word and provide examples of scientific theories. In Lesson 3.3, students will assess claims and evaluate their veracity by looking for support, and then rewrite the claims, if needed, using evidence.

LESSON 3.1

ANALYZING CLAIMS

RESOURCES AND MATERIALS

- Lesson 3.1 Evaluating Claims in Advertisements
- Lesson 3.1 Testing Advertisement Claims
- Advertisements (hard copies and online examples to be projected on the board)

ESTIMATED TIME

1 hour

OBJECTIVE

In this lesson, students will:
- evaluate and analyze claims in advertisements, and
- understand the connection between claims and evidence.

CONTENT

Students will analyze advertisements, particularly those targeting them, and determine the claims that are being made. For example, currently there are many ads for e-cigarettes targeting young people. These ads commonly depict this type of smoking as "healthier" than smoking traditional cigarettes. Using the scientific skills of observation, questioning, and testing, students can begin to develop an inquiry-based investigation about the claims of advertisements directed at them.

PRIOR KNOWLEDGE

Students should understand that claims must be supported by evidence. They may have some difficulty with the vocabulary in the advertisements, but they can use the context of the advertisement to arrive at the meaning of an unfamiliar word.

INSTRUCTIONAL SEQUENCE

1. Project an advertisement relevant to the students' age group on the board. For example, when searching for advertisements that target teens online, one can find advertisements claiming that e-cigarettes are as healthy as fresh fruit. Have students examine the advertisement. Then, elicit responses: *What is the claim that is made in the advertisement? Is there any support for this claim?* Remind students that claims may be explicitly written or subtly suggested through images.
2. Divide students into groups of 2–3. Distribute hard copies of advertisements intended for the age group of your students. You may gather these ads before the lesson or ask students to bring in advertisements from home. Be sure to preview the advertisements before using them in the lesson.
3. Distribute Lesson 3.1 Evaluating Claims in Advertisements. Have groups examine the claims made in the advertisements and assess the veracity of the claims.
4. When students have completed their analysis, discuss the results with the class.
5. Guide students to consider how one might test advertisement claims. Distribute Lesson 3.1 Testing Advertisement Claims for students to complete.
6. Ask students: *How would you test the claims you found in your advertisement? What kind of experiment would you design?*

EXTENSION ACTIVITIES

- Have students rewrite the packaging of the product on the basis of their analysis of the claim and the evidence provided for it.
- Have students analyze several advertisement claims, using a Venn diagram to compare and contrast their findings.

ASSESSMENT OBSERVATIONS

- Students should identify the claims made in the advertisements.
- Students should find evidence to support or refute those claims.

LESSON 3.1

Evaluating Claims in Advertisements

Directions: With your group, examine the advertisement and answer the following questions.

1. What is the claim?

2. What evidence is there to support the claim?

3. What sources can be used to support or refute the claim?

4. Is the claim supported with evidence? Why or why not?

LESSON 3.1

Testing Advertisement Claims

Directions: Consider the following scenario and answer the questions about the resulting experiment.

Ann reached for a cookie and noticed an interesting claim on its wrapper: "Provides you with 5 hours of energy!" Ann looked at the ingredients and wondered if this could be true. She showed the wrapper to her science teacher and asked if she could test this claim using her classmates as subjects.

To conduct the experiment, Ann had all of her classmates take a survey about their energy levels and then offered the experimental group the cookies with 5 hours of energy. The other group of students received similar-looking cookies with no energy-boosting claims. Five hours later, the class answered survey questions about their energy levels.

1. Why is it important to have a group of students receive the non-energy cookies?

2. The students who had the energy cookies reported having 30% more energy than those who had the regular cookies. What conclusions can Ann make?

3. How could Ann improve her experiment?

4. How do you think the energy cookie company came up with the claim of "Provides you with 5 hours of energy!"?

LESSON 3.2

THEORIES ARE LIKE PUZZLES

RESOURCES AND MATERIALS

- Lesson 3.2 Puzzle Pieces (teacher use; cardstock may be used as a base to reinforce the pieces)
- Lesson 3.2 Theory Puzzle Reflection

ESTIMATED TIME

1 hour

OBJECTIVES

In this lesson, students will:
- differentiate the scientific use of the word *theory* from the everyday use of the word, and
- provide examples of scientific theories.

CONTENT

The denotation of *theory* in science differs greatly from its general usage. Students need to know that a scientific theory is much more substantial than simply a "guess." In science, the word *theory* means that a phenomenon can be explained using scientific evidence from experiments. A theory is formulated from the evidence, inferences, and conclusions based on experimentation. Hypotheses derived from a theory can be tested. A theory can also be modified based on additional information or interpretation.

PRIOR KNOWLEDGE

Students should have a basic understanding of the term *theory* (e.g., the Big Bang Theory).

INSTRUCTIONAL SEQUENCE

1. To introduce this activity, explain to students that scientific theories are based on ideas supported by evidence. A theory is like a puzzle; each puzzle piece lends support by explaining part of the theory. Help students to differentiate the everyday use of the word *theory* from the scientific use of it (i.e., everyday usage does not necessarily rely on evidence).

2. Give each group of 2–3 students four pieces of the puzzle from Lesson 3.2 Puzzle Pieces (all pieces except the "x" piece). Tell students that each of the four pieces represents a component of a scientific theory. They must work to connect the pieces into a square, or a coherent theory. To make the puzzle configuration more contextualized, use a specific theory, such as the Theory of Plate Tectonics, and write the evidence for the theory on each puzzle piece before the lesson. Other possible theories to use for this activity include evolution and the Big Bang Theory.

3. Have students work to fit the puzzle pieces together in a square, forming a coherent theory (see Figure 1). Explain that they have just fit all of the components of the theory together.

4. Then, explain that there is new knowledge to incorporate into this theory (i.e., a scientist has discovered something new). This new knowledge is represented by a small square, marked with an "x." Pass out the "x" squares to each group and ask students to reassemble the first "theory" they constructed, incorporating the new "knowledge" (see Figure 2). As with the first four pieces, consider writing the new knowledge on the puzzle piece before the lesson. For example, if you are using the Theory of Plate Tectonics, you might use Hess's discovery of seafloor spreading for the "x" piece.

5. After students have reconfigured their puzzles, distribute Lesson 3.2 Theory Puzzle Reflection. Students may answer individually, in groups, or through a class discussion. Guide them to understand that the additional puzzle piece represents tangible evidence that theories can evolve with new data.

6. Discuss with the class how scientific knowledge evolves and incorporates new knowledge and discovery. You might incorporate new scientific findings into the science content being taught. For example, if the class is learning about the formation of our solar system, you might mention that a recent finding about diamonds in meteorites lends support to the theory of an early Earth collision, which helped form the moon.

Figure 1. Four-piece coherent theory puzzle. From "'The Nature of Science': An Activity for the First Day of Class" by J. Choi, 2004. Reprinted with permission of the author.

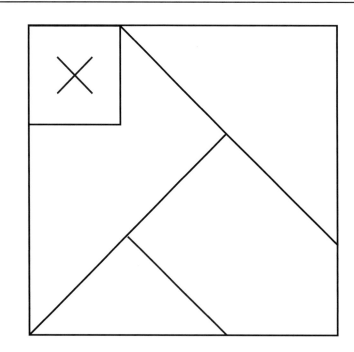

Figure 2. Coherent theory puzzle with additional knowledge. From "The Nature of Science: An Activity for the First Day of Class" by J. Choi, 2004. Reprinted with permission of the author.

EXTENSION ACTIVITY

Have students investigate the formation of the theory used in the puzzle activity. They might look more closely at the historical development of that particular theory. In the example of plate tectonics, students first might research Alfred Wegener, who proposed the theory of continental drift in 1912. Wegener's evidence for this theory included observational evidence, such as the puzzle fit of continents and the matching rock formations and fossils on different continents. At that time, however, he could not provide the evidence for the mechanism underlying the theory of continental drift. His theory, therefore, was deemed controversial. It was not until 1950 that Harry Hess, a U.S. Navy Captain, formulated the theory of seafloor spreading. Hess used sonar to make ocean floor profiles and found mid-ocean ridges formed by diverging ocean plates. This was the mechanism that Wegener had needed to complete his theory. Today students learn that both continental drift and seafloor spreading are the integral components that comprise the Theory of Plate Tectonics.

ASSESSMENT OBSERVATION

Have students reflect on the following in their science notebooks: *How does the puzzle theory activity relate to the nature of science?* Students should provide illustrative examples of the nature of science in their written explanation.

Puzzle Pieces

Teacher directions: Cut out the puzzle pieces for each group to use with the lesson. If you would like to connect this activity to a particular theory, write out the components of the theory on each piece. The "x" piece should be reserved for a later discovery that changed scientists' understanding of the theory.

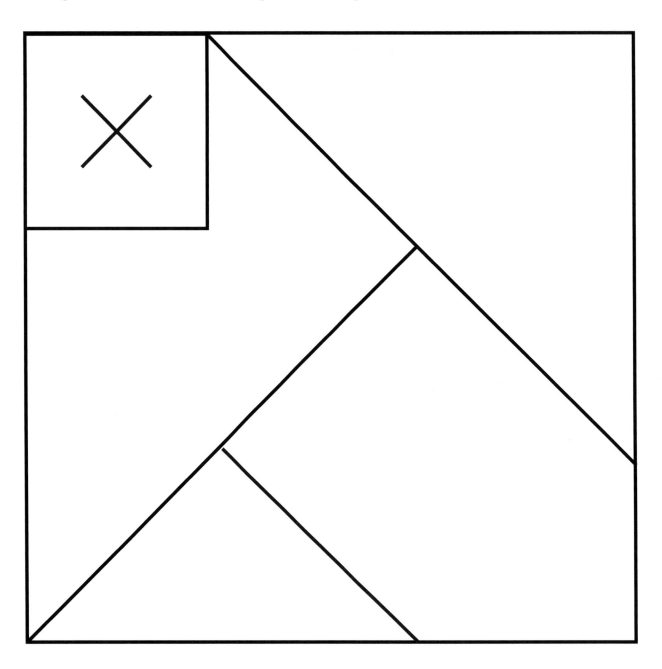

Note. From "'The Nature of Science': An Activity for the First Day of Class" by J. Choi, 2004. Reprinted with permission of the author.

LESSON 3.2
Theory Puzzle Reflection

Directions: Complete the following reflection questions about your theory puzzle.

1. How do scientists make sense of new discoveries?

2. Were you able to assemble the puzzle into a square the first time you tried it? What does that tell you about the necessity of repeated trials?

3. What did you have to do to your first "theory" (first finished puzzle) after you received a new piece of knowledge? What does this tell you about the nature of science?

4. What other theories have undergone changes over the years based on new discoveries?

LESSON 3.3

UNCOVERING MISCONCEPTIONS

RESOURCES AND MATERIALS

- Lesson 3.3 Uncovering Misconceptions

ESTIMATED TIME

One class period

OBJECTIVES

In this lesson, students will
- assess claims and evaluate their veracity by looking for support, and
- rewrite the claims, if needed, using evidence.

CONTENT

In science, it is important to correct misconceptions. Students will learn from this activity that claims must be supported by evidence.

PRIOR KNOWLEDGE

Students have probably heard the misconceptions used in this lesson, but they may not recognize them as misconceptions.

INSTRUCTIONAL SEQUENCE

1. Explain: *Evaluating ideas and theories is inherent in the practice of science. Scientists do not "prove" claims; rather claims and hypotheses are supported by evidence gained from valid experiments. A theory is backed by evidence, and new evidence may refute a previously supported idea.*

2. Elicit responses to the question "Why is the sky blue?" Record each response on the board. There may be a variety of responses.

3. Ask the class for ways to find support for some of the claims that students made for why the sky is blue. Students may suggest the Internet, the library, or textbooks.

4. Distribute Lesson 3.3 Uncovering Misconceptions. Instruct students to work in pairs to read the sentences, investigate the claims, and decide if evidence supports them.

5. Discuss follow-up questions: *How do you find out if these claims are supported by evidence? How can you know if the source's evidence is verifiable?* It is important to convey that questioning all aspects of a claim is a science practice.

EXTENSION ACTIVITIES

*   Have students respond to the following in their science notebooks: *Write about a personal experience when you uncovered a misconception. What happened next? How did your thinking change?*
*   Have students create a short picture book for a younger audience, explaining the misconceptions from Lesson 3.3 Uncovering Misconceptions.

ASSESSMENT OBSERVATIONS

*   Students should provide evidence for each correction of the misconceptions.
*   Students should be able to explain the evidence for why the misconceptions are wrong.

LESSON 3.3

Uncovering Misconceptions

Directions: Determine whether each claim is a misconception or a fact. For each misconception, you and your partner will use a source to find support for the statement or find evidence to correct the statement. Make sure you provide the evidence in your own words.

Claim	Misconception or Fact?	Evidence
The sky is blue because it reflects the ocean.		
Your body's blood is blue before it reaches your lungs.		
Air has mass.		
Seasons are the result of Earth's tilt and Earth's varying distance in its elliptical orbit around the sun.		
Our atmosphere is 100% oxygen.		
Most earthquakes happen near plate boundaries.		

UNIT 4
WHAT IS CRITICAL THINKING?

RATIONALE

Data literacy is a vital component of critical thinking skills through which students can become confident in their use of data. Students will develop several critical thinking skills in this unit by engaging in science: inductive reasoning, deductive reasoning, and abductive reasoning. *Inductive reasoning* is built upon an example leading to a larger premise. For example, the statement "The plants in my garden have roots. Therefore, all plants have roots" begins with an observation, which leads to a generalized claim. *Deductive reasoning*, however, is considered scientific reasoning. With deductive reasoning, one uses a theory to make hypotheses and then tests these hypotheses through experimentation. The wild card of scientific reasoning is *abductive reasoning*. Scientists often operate on incomplete or elusive evidence. Incomplete fossil evidence and hypothesized components of string theory require the creativity and imagination of scientists as they try to make sense of phenomena.

PLAN

In Lesson 4.1, students will use the I^2 strategy to identify and interpret what they see in graphs so that they can form accurate statements about graphs. In Lesson 4.2, students will analyze articles and experiments using the Claim-Evidence-Reasoning strategy and template. In Lesson 4.3, students will devise models of Earth motions. In Lesson 4.4, students will engineer boats made from aluminum foil.

LESSON 4.1

USING THE I² STRATEGY

RESOURCES AND MATERIALS

- Line graphs and bar graphs related to content taught in class; these can be created before class using Microsoft Excel
- Model of I² Strategy projected on board (see https://media.bscs.org/icans/Icans_I2_SE.pdf for an example)
- Handheld whiteboards, markers, and erasers

ESTIMATED TIME

One class period

OBJECTIVES

In this lesson, students will:
- identify and interpret graphs using the I² Strategy, and
- write captions for graphs using the I² Strategy.

CONTENT

The Identify and Interpret (I²) strategy, developed by the Biological Sciences Curriculum Study (BSCS, 2012), is a means by which students break down the components of a visual representation in order to grasp its meaning. By analyzing a graph or chart in smaller components, students can derive greater meaning and draw conclusions from it more successfully. For more information about I², see https://media.bscs.org/icans/Icans_I2_SE.pdf

PRIOR KNOWLEDGE

Students should have experience interpreting graphs and charts in science class, as well as in other classes. They should have experience making their own graphs and charts.

INSTRUCTIONAL SEQUENCE

1. Create or use a graph related to unit content that students are currently studying. Project the graph and ask students to identify what they see.
2. After the class has identified the major aspects of the graph, introduce the I² Strategy to students. Explain the process that students will use to interpret the graph (see Figure 3 for an example graph with student responses):
   - **Identify:** Students will write "what I see" statements on the board.
   - **Interpret:** Students will write "what it means" statements on the board.
   - **Caption:** Students will create a caption explaining the graph by connecting the "what I see" and "what it means" statements.

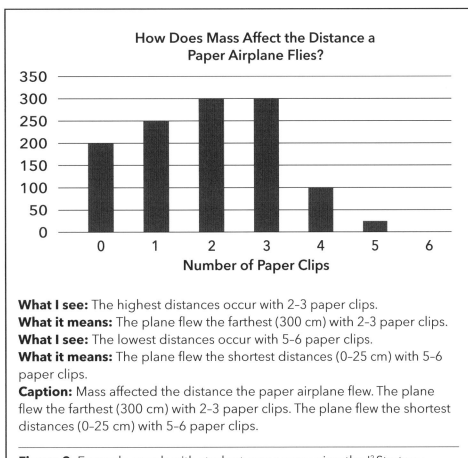

What I see: The highest distances occur with 2–3 paper clips.
What it means: The plane flew the farthest (300 cm) with 2–3 paper clips.
What I see: The lowest distances occur with 5–6 paper clips.
What it means: The plane flew the shortest distances (0–25 cm) with 5–6 paper clips.
Caption: Mass affected the distance the paper airplane flew. The plane flew the farthest (300 cm) with 2–3 paper clips. The plane flew the shortest distances (0–25 cm) with 5–6 paper clips.

Figure 3. Example graph with student responses using the I² Strategy.

3. Divide students into pairs. Provide a graph for each group and instruct students to use the I^2 Strategy to analyze the graphs on their handheld whiteboards.

4. When all groups have completed their analyses, each group should present its graphs to the class.

EXTENSION ACTIVITY

Ask students to find a graph used in another class or seen in the news. Students can use the I^2 Strategy to analyze and write a caption for the graph.

ASSESSMENT OBSERVATIONS

- Students should be able to identify the independent and dependent variables and interpret the relationship between the two.
- Students should be able to combine the identification ("what I see") and interpretation ("what it means") to form a coherent caption for the graph.

LESSON 4.2

DEEP THINKING USING CLAIM, EVIDENCE, AND REASONING

RESOURCES AND MATERIALS

- Lesson 4.2 Claim-Evidence-Reasoning Template
- Web article: "Enormous Floating Barrier Will Corral Ocean Trash" by Carolyn Gramling at https://www.sciencenewsforstudents.org/article/enormous-floating-barrier-will-corral-ocean-trash
- Other science news articles from books or online; timely articles can be found at https://www.sciencenewsforstudents.org

ESTIMATED TIME

One class period

OBJECTIVES

In this lesson, students will
- engage in deep thinking, and
- analyze scientific articles and experiments, using the Claim-Evidence-Reasoning (CER) handout.

CONTENT

The Claim-Evidence-Reasoning (CER) template can be used by students to analyze science articles and identify the underlying scientific reasoning. Analyzing and evaluating scientific claims develops critical thinking skills needed for science in students.

The critical thinking skills applied to visual representations of data using the I^2 strategy (see Lesson 4.1) are vital to understanding science and can be furthered through writing scientific explanations based on research. When students are given science articles to read, they are tasked with identifying the research question, stating the claim, providing evidence, and using reasoning to support the claim. A basic CER template includes the following components.

- **Research Question:** What is the purpose of the article or experiment?
- **Claim:** Respond to the research question with a statement.
- **Evidence:** How do the data support the claim?
- **Reasoning:** Why do the data support the evidence? How can you link the evidence to the claim?

PRIOR KNOWLEDGE

Students will have read science news articles and experiments. They may have experience answering questions about these texts.

INSTRUCTIONAL SEQUENCE

1. Present students with the article "Enormous Floating Barrier Will Corral Ocean Trash" or another current news article related to the topic of the unit being studied. Any relevant grade 5 topic will work well for this lesson.
2. As this particular article is intended for middle/high school students and includes a list of vocabulary words and definitions, have students read the article on their own first. Remind students to highlight the main idea and supporting details.
3. Elicit responses to help students understand the article. Some guiding questions include: *What is the intended purpose of the ocean cleanup? How will it work? What are the advantages of this project? What are some possible disadvantages?*
4. Distribute Lesson 4.2 Claim-Evidence-Reasoning Template and review it with students, discussing research questions, claims, evidence, and reasoning. Students should complete the template using the article discussed in class.
5. Have students work with partners to review their responses. Students should work together to make sure that they have identified the claim that the article is stating. It is important for students to realize that their claims can be expressed using different words, but all of the claims should have the same meaning.
6. Once students are done reviewing, ask: *How can this strategy help you better understand information? How could you use this strategy when planning and conducting experiments?*
7. Assign additional articles for students to analyze using the CER strategy. These articles may be analyzed inside or outside of class.

EXTENSION ACTIVITIES

- Assign weekly science news articles and ask students to complete Lesson 4.2 Claim-Evidence-Reasoning Template for each article.
- Provide students with an incomplete graph, such as the one shown in Figure 4, in which the title and percentages are absent from the pie chart. Ask students to deduce and extrapolate the information, and then add a title. If students are aware that a whole pie chart represents 100%, they will be able to derive approximate percentages for the color-coded elements. If students have learned about meteorology, they might correctly guess the title. If not, they should create a title based on what they do know.

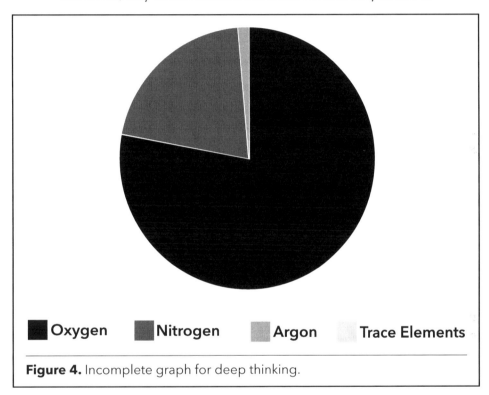

Oxygen   **Nitrogen**   **Argon**   **Trace Elements**

Figure 4. Incomplete graph for deep thinking.

ASSESSMENT OBSERVATION

Students may find themselves copying text in order to avoid mistakes. Let students know that the classroom is a safe place to learn how to paraphrase and that mistakes are expected.

LESSON 4.2

Claim-Evidence-Reasoning Template

Directions: Complete this template to analyze an article or experiment. The *claim* is a statement about the results of an experiment or a scientific phenomenon. The *evidence* is data used to support the claim. The *reasoning* is the understanding that connects the claim and evidence.

Research Question What is the purpose of the article or experiment?	
Claim Respond to the research question with a statement.	
Evidence How do the data support the claim?	
Reasoning Why do the data support the evidence? How can you link the evidence to the claim?	

LESSON 4.3

PROJECT: MAKING MODELS OF EARTH MOTIONS

RESOURCES AND MATERIALS

- Lesson 4.3 KWL Earth Motions
- Lesson 4.3 Rubric
- Materials for modeling Earth motion (e.g., Styrofoam balls, straws, cups, flashlights, etc.)

ESTIMATED TIME

1 hour

OBJECTIVE

In this lesson, students will:
- construct models of Earth's motions, and
- justify how these models represent Earth's motion.

CONTENT

When students engage in model-making, they are putting their critical thinking skills to use. Making models not only engages students visually and kinesthetically, but also intellectually. Earth position and motions is a grade 5 standard that is ideal for modeling.

PRIOR KNOWLEDGE

Students should be able to differentiate rotation from revolution.

INSTRUCTIONAL SEQUENCE

1. To determine student understanding and interest level, distribute Lesson 4.3 KWL Earth Motions for students to complete. Students will fill in the "K" ("What I Know") column and the "W" ("What I Want to Learn") column. Hold a class discussion about students' understanding of Earth motions.

2. Explain to students the importance of models: Model-making makes the intangible tangible. When phenomena are uncontrollable, such as a cyclone, or elusive, such as cosmic background radiation, scientists can use physical and computational models to study these phenomena.

3. Divide students into groups and supply them with clearly defined group roles to investigate assigned topics, such as lunar phases, Earth's rotation, or Earth's revolution:
   - **Leader:** Keeps everyone on task and delegates responsibility
   - **Time keeper:** Makes sure the task is done on time
   - **Presenter:** Gives a summary of the ideas discussed to the class
   - **Recorder:** Takes notes on the group discussion

4. Have students research the assigned topic and work on devising a model to show the effects of Earth's position or motions. Each component of the model should represent some facet of the natural processes being modeled.

5. Each group will give a presentation to the class about its Earth motion or position topic and explain its model to the class (see Lesson 4.3 Rubric).

6. Students can now complete the "L" portion, of the KWL Chart: "What I Learned." Answers can be shared as a group or displayed in a designated area in the classroom for others to read.

EXTENSION ACTIVITY

Have students use their models of Earth's motion to teach younger students. Younger students could circulate through stations at which the grade 5 students demonstrate and explain their models.

ASSESSMENT OBSERVATIONS

- Students should use creativity and abductive reasoning to make their models.
- Students should experiment using trial and error.
- Students should design a model to best represent rotation and revolution.

LESSON 4.3

KWL Earth Motions

Directions: Complete the KWL chart about Earth's motions. Complete the "K" and "W" columns before the activity. You will complete the "L" column after you have completed the activity.

K	W	L
What do you think you know about Earth's position and motions?	What do you want to learn about Earth's position and motions?	What have you learned about Earth's position and motions?

LESSON 4.3
Rubric

	4	3	2	1
Information	The student's finished product shows evidence of all of the resources. The facts are presented coherently in the final product.	The student's finished product shows evidence of most of the resources. The facts are presented mostly coherently in the final product.	The student's finished product shows evidence of some of the resources. The facts are presented somewhat coherently in the final product.	The student's finished product shows evidence of none of the resources. The facts are not presented coherently in the final product.
Model	The model accurately portrays the intended Earth motion. The student can explain the model and the motion, showing a great depth of understanding.	The model mostly portrays the intended Earth motion. The student can mostly explain the model and the motion, showing a depth of understanding.	The model somewhat portrays the intended Earth motion. The student can somewhat explain the model and the motion, showing some understanding.	The model does not portray the intended Earth motion. The student cannot explain the model and the motion, showing no understanding.
Mechanics	The student confidently explains the model with few or no hesitations. The model functions as intended.	The student can explain the model with a few hesitations. The model mostly functions as intended.	The student can somewhat explain the model with multiple hesitations. The model somewhat functions as intended.	The student cannot explain the model unless reading from notes. The model does not function as intended.

LESSON 4.4

PROJECT: ENGINEERING A BOAT

RESOURCES AND MATERIALS

- Lesson 4.4 Designing a Boat With Aluminum Foil
- Materials for creating and testing boats (per group of three):
  - 3 sheets of aluminum foil, 12 cm x 12 cm each
  - 50 pennies
  - Small container of water on which to test the boats

ESTIMATED TIME

1 hour

OBJECTIVES

In this lesson, students will:
- collaborate to engineer an aluminum foil boat that will hold pennies, and
- assess the efficacy of each boat by testing designs and devising means to improve them.

CONTENT

Objects that are more dense than water (greater than 1.0 g/mL) sink, while objects that are less dense than water float. However, by manipulating surface area, students can design a boat to float and hold pennies.

PRIOR KNOWLEDGE

Students should have a basic understanding of density by grade 5. To review, display a bottle of oil and vinegar salad dressing and ask students why the bottle states "Shake Well Before Using." The students will be able to clearly see the oil layered on top of the vinegar, demonstrating different densities of liquids.

INSTRUCTIONAL SEQUENCE

1. To introduce this activity, ask for examples of things that float on water and what they illustrate about density. Ask: *Who can float on water? What can you tell about the density of the human body (0.98 g/mL) compared to that of water?*
2. Tell students that they will be designing boats made of aluminum foil to hold as many pennies as possible. Students will work together in groups of three to record their designs as well as how each design fared when tested.
3. Present each group of students with three pieces of precut foil, Lesson 4.4 Designing a Boat With Aluminum Foil, a small container of water, and 50 pennies. Have students create and test their first boat.
4. After groups have tested their first boat, ask questions to help them improve their designs. Some questions to ask include:
   - Your boat floated and held four pennies. What could you do to improve the design to allow it to hold more pennies?
   - What could you do to prevent your boat from sagging in the middle?

5. When all groups have finished testing their three designs, ask which design held the most pennies. Ask the group responsible for that design to discuss why that boat held the greatest number of pennies.
6. In their groups, have students discuss and answer the analysis questions on Lesson 4.4 Engineering a Boat With Aluminum Foil.
7. When all students have finished responding to the analysis questions, invite different groups to share their responses to the questions. Discuss with the class how advances in science come about through collaboration and testing of ideas.

EXTENSION ACTIVITIES

- In their science notebooks, have students respond to the following quote by Thomas Edison: "Genius is one percent inspiration, ninety-nine percent perspiration." Students should give examples of how they worked hard to achieve a result or solve a difficult problem.
- If students are motivated to design more boats, they can try using other materials, such as clay or playdough.
- Have students research Archimedes' Principle and find examples of water displacement around them.

ASSESSMENT OBSERVATIONS

- Students should be able to work together and carry out the assigned engineering task.
- Students should collaborate on design improvement.
- Students should be able to explain why testing and evaluating results are crucial to advances in scientific knowledge.

LESSON 4.4
Designing a Boat With Aluminum Foil

Directions: How do you design a boat out of a material that is more dense than water? In this activity, you will use pieces of aluminum foil, which has a density of 2.70 g/mL, to design three boats to float on water and hold as many pennies as possible. For each design that you and your group create, please record the following information.

Boat design	Sketch of boat design	How many pennies do you think it will hold?	How many pennies did your boat hold?	Ideas for improving the boat design
1				
2				
3				

Designing a Boat With Aluminum Foil, continued

Analysis Questions

1. How did your group use the first boat design to improve the following boat designs? Please give examples.

2. What other factors (besides the design) allowed your boats to hold pennies? Please give examples.

3. How can a substance such as aluminum foil, which has a density of 2.70 g/mL, float on water, which has a density of 1.0 g/mL?

4. Why is it important to keep trying to improve the boat design?

5. Which group's boat held the most pennies? How did its design allow it to hold the most pennies?

UNIT 5
PUTTING SCIENTIFIC SKILLS TO USE

RATIONALE

What do your students know about the practice of science? There is no better way to find out than by having them do their own research. Student-directed research not only leaves lasting impressions, but also has a major impact on how students regard themselves as scientists. They learn that most scientific research is long-term and requires many trials. Student scientists will face frequent setbacks and reconsiderations of original plans.

Before you plan research projects for students, there are several questions to consider:

- How much time do we have? What is the timeline for the project?
- Is there an established project in the community we could work with?
- Should this be a class project, a small-group project, or an individual science fair project?
- If this is a group project, how will roles be equitably defined?
- What resources are needed?
- Will there be any digital images of students or others used? If so, what must be done for permission?
- Does the school district require students to obtain permission before conducting research?
- Will students be presenting the project to an outside audience?

Group projects are ideal for students when they have a set-aside time, such as a gifted resource period, during which they can collaborate on the implementation of the project. An afterschool science club is another opportune setting for a group project. If students are in a general classroom setting, consider if and how to best group students.

PLAN

In Lesson 5.1, students will work in groups to construct and test solar ovens. In Lesson 5.2, students will carry out investigations using the controlled environment of terrariums. In Lesson 5.3, students will participate as members of a class research team collaborating on an investigation. All of these projects are long-term (i.e., lasting more than a week) and require collaboration among students.

LESSON 5.1

PROJECT: SOLAR OVEN CONSTRUCTION

RESOURCES AND MATERIALS

- Lesson 5.1 KWL Solar Ovens
- Lesson 5.1 Experimental Design
- Web resources:
    - Article: "Sunny Science: Build a Pizza Box Solar Oven" by Science Buddies (https://www.scientificamerican.com/article/sunny-science-build-a-pizza-box-solar-oven)
    - Video: "Solar Cooking" by National Geographic (https://www.youtube.com/watch?v=Ofn7jqPDTeY)

- Outdoor area with adequate sunlight
- Solar oven materials:
    - Clean pizza boxes (one per group)
    - Box cutter
    - Aluminum foil
    - Plastic wrap
    - Tape
    - Black paper (half of the class will line their boxes with black paper)
    - White paper (the other half will line their boxes with white paper)
    - Ingredients for s'mores (marshmallows, graham crackers, and chocolate)
    - Thermometers and stop watches

ESTIMATED TIME

One week

OBJECTIVES

In this lesson, students will:
- demonstrate proficiency in the scientific method, and
- participate in and carry out a long-term scientific research project.

CONTENT

Students will follow the steps of the scientific method while carrying out an investigation involving solar energy. This is a highly relevant research topic as many environmentally conscious people and governments seek the use of alternatives to fossil fuels.

PRIOR KNOWLEDGE

Students may be familiar with solar ovens. If not, provide students with background information or have students research solar ovens online (see Resources and Materials).

INSTRUCTIONAL SEQUENCE

1. Prepare the boxes before class. To make the solar ovens, cut a flap in the top of each pizza box, leaving a 1" margin around the flap (see Figure 5).
2. Distribute Lesson 5.1 KWL Solar Ovens. Students should complete the "K" and the "W" columns of the KWL chart.
3. Show the video "Solar Cooking" to students. Allow students to edit their KWL charts with new information.
4. Divide students into groups of 3–4. Each group should receive a pizza box with a precut flap in the top (see Step 1).
5. Students can complete the ovens by using tape to secure plastic wrap in the window under the flap and lining the inside of the box and the flap with aluminum foil (see Figure 5).
6. Distribute a sheet of either black or white paper to each group to place at the bottom of their boxes. One group should receive no paper (this unlined box will serve as the control).
7. Some questions to ask during box construction might include:
   - What do you think the effect of the silver foil will be? How do you know?
   - How do you think the temperatures might differ depending on the color of the paper (black, white, or no paper)? How do you know?

Figure 5. Solar pizza oven example.

8. When students have completed their ovens, have them place a thermometer on the black or white paper or the unlined box. They should then assemble a s'more and place it in the center of the box.

9. Have the class place the boxes in a sunny area. Students should make sure all boxes have the same amount of sunlight and are facing the same direction.

10. Instruct students to check the temperature every 5 minutes using a stopwatch and record the temperature in their science notebooks. Have them continue doing so until the boxes have heated sufficiently (the total length of time will depend on the outdoor temperature).

11. During the 5-minute waiting increments, have groups work together to complete Lesson 5.1 Experimental Design.

12. Some questions to ask during the experiment include:
    - What might be causing the temperature differences between the black and white squares?
    - What is the function of the plastic wrap?
    - What is the solar oven modeling? (The solar oven is an example of heat transfer by convection.)

13. Some questions to ask after the experiment include:
    - What was the importance of having the oven facing direct light?
    - How might cloud coverage or the time of day affect your data?
    - What are some ways your group might improve on this solar oven design?

14. Have students complete the "L" portion of their KWL charts. Allow students to share them with the class or display the charts in an assigned area in the classroom.

EXTENSION ACTIVITIES

- Have students work in small groups to design another solar oven, taking into account the location and time of year. How might a solar oven be designed for locations at high latitudes (with greater variability in amount of sunlight) and high altitudes (with less air pressure)? How might a solar oven be designed for winter use?
- Have students design a model that can sustain the highest temperature for the longest time. Set up a competition for students to design solar ovens that sustain high temperatures long enough to completely bake something (e.g., premade cookie dough).
- If students are fascinated by solar ovens, introduce them to solar oven recipes (https://www.homesciencetools.com/content/reference/SolarOvenRecipes.pdf) and solar oven designs (http://solarcooking.org/plans).

ASSESSMENT OBSERVATIONS

- Students should be actively engaged in all aspects of this long-term project.
- Students should be able to support claims made pertaining to this experiment with evidence.
- The solar oven they design should be based on the efficiency of the first oven, and they should be able to justify its design to the class.

NAME: _____ DATE: _____

LESSON 5.1
KWL Solar Ovens

Directions: Complete the "K" and "W" columns in the chart. You will add to this chart once you have learned more about the topic.

K	W	L
What do you think you know about solar ovens?	What do you want to learn about solar ovens?	What have you learned about solar ovens?

LESSON 5.1

Experimental Design

Directions: Define the parts of your solar oven experiment with your group members, using the chart below.

Independent Variable	
Dependent Variable	
Constants	
Control Group	
Hypothesis	

Experimental Design, continued

Materials	
Procedure	
Data	
Analysis	
Conclusion	
Future Experiments	

LESSON 5.2

PROJECT: TESTING IN TERRARIUMS

RESOURCES AND MATERIALS

- Lesson 5.2 Water Cycle
- Lesson 5.2 Terrarium Investigation
- Terrarium materials (per student)
  - Large glass jar with lid (an empty pickle jar works well)
  - Sterilized potting soil
  - Activated charcoal or small pebbles
  - Water
  - Small plants or seeds
  - Ruler
  - An area with adequate sunlight for the plants to grow

ESTIMATED TIME

Set-up time: One class period. After setting up the terrarium, students can monitor the variables they choose to study on a daily or weekly basis.

OBJECTIVES

In this lesson, students will:
- create a model of the water cycle using a terrarium,
- devise tests to assess how the water cycle works, and
- demonstrate accurate record-keeping of the quantitative and qualitative variables they study.

CONTENT

There are many cycles in nature, such as the water cycle, that are so massive and unwieldy that a smaller model, such as terrarium, facilitates a better opportunity for the study of these cycles. Models are often used to study scientific phenomena, such as hurricanes and tornadoes.

PRIOR KNOWLEDGE

Students should have seen small-scale models of large-scale objects, such as maps. They may need clarification on how models help scientists focus on specific scientific interests without the interference of other variables. For example, a student wanting to model convection can add cold food coloring to a clear bowl of hot water in order to view convection clearly without the interference of other variables.

INSTRUCTIONAL SEQUENCE

1. Before the lesson, create a model terrarium with the same materials students will be using (see Step 2 for directions). Show students the model terrarium and ask the following questions to guide a discussion about how the terrarium can model the water cycle:
   - How will these plants get water?
   - How did the water get under the lid?
   - Why is water on the inside of the jar?
   - What part of the water cycle does that show?
   - Will we have to water these plants?
   - What role do plants play in the water cycle? (Transpiration.)
   - How could this terrarium give us information about the role of plants in the water cycle?

2. Provide the materials for the terrarium construction and make sure that the glass jars cannot be dropped or broken. Have students begin creating their terrariums.
   - Add 2 inches of activated charcoal (to minimize smells) or pebbles to the bottom of the jar for drainage.
   - Add at least 5–8 inches of sterilized potting soil.
   - Plant small plants, such as ferns or moss, in the soil.
   - Water the plants; enough water to moisten the soil is all that is needed.
   - Place a lid on the jar and move the terrarium to a location with plenty of sunlight.

3. Distribute Lesson 5.2 Water Cycle for students to complete individually. Circulate among students in order to answer or ask questions. The last

question will require students to change one variable of their terrariums and then record their observations over a 5-day or 5-week period.

4. When students have completed their observations, distribute Lesson 5.2 Terrarium Investigation to help students reflect and prepare to present their findings to the class.

5. Have students present their findings to the class in a gallery walk. Half the class will remain by their terrariums with their handouts (see Lesson 5.2 Terrarium Investigation), while the other half visits the students and their terrariums. After a specified time, have students switch roles. As students visit other terrariums, they should ask questions and give comments regarding the terrariums.

6. As a closure to this investigation, have students contribute to a discussion, indicating what they learned from their investigations.

7. In their science notebooks, have students write about how their models and their manipulation of one variable reflect the water cycle.

EXTENSION ACTIVITIES

- Have students develop their investigation into an experiment.
- Extend the investigation by asking students to continue to maintain accurate data, both quantitative and qualitative, on their terrariums over the rest of the school year.

ASSESSMENT OBSERVATIONS

- Students should be able explain the water cycle they have observed in their terrariums.
- Students should be able to assess the relevance of the terrarium to model the water cycle.
- Students should be to maintain ongoing records of data for the duration of the "Testing in Terrariums" project.

LESSON 5.2
Water Cycle

Directions: Please complete the following handout with information about your terrarium and what you can learn from it.

1. Use your textbook or online sources to draw a picture of the water cycle below. Make sure you include the role of plants in the water cycle.

Water Cycle, continued

2. Now draw the water cycle you see going on within your terrarium. Make sure you label the parts of the water cycle.

Thinking Like a Scientist © Prufrock Press Inc.

Water Cycle, continued

3. Think about what might happen if you changed one variable in your terrarium after you have observed your terrarium for several days. Some variables you can change are amount of sunlight, amount of water, temperature, number of plants, or removing the lid. Choose one of these variables to manipulate. Then, make regular (daily or weekly) observations of what you witness happening.

Day 1 Observations:

Day 2 Observations:

Day 3 Observations:

Day 4 Observations:

Day 5 Observations:

LESSON 5.2
Terrarium Investigation

Directions: Please complete the following questions about your terrarium investigation. You will use this information to present your terrarium in a gallery walk.

Question	Response
How did your terrarium model the water cycle?	
What variable did you change in your terrarium?	
Why did you change this variable?	
What were some of your observations after you changed this variable?	
What would happen if this change occurred in the global water cycle?	
What are some things you wonder about as you see other students' terrarium investigations?	

LESSON 5.3

PROJECT: WORKING IN RESEARCH TEAMS

RESOURCES AND MATERIALS

- Lesson 5.3 Team Research Project
- Student computers with Microsoft Excel
- Materials to create the projects (will vary, depending on class choice)

ESTIMATED TIME

One class period; then ongoing, based on classroom needs

OBJECTIVES

In this lesson, students will:
- plan and create a research project as a large group, and
- implement the project by working together.

CONTENT

When conducting research as a class or in small groups, students learn the importance of collaboration with others. When the small groups report the findings of their research and experiments, other students can glean information to build future experiments. Students also learn essential interpersonal skills, such as delegating responsibility and politely disagreeing with others. They must work together to sort out the procedural and logistical information of the experimental method. Good data are essential if students want to have experimental support, and good data are the result of very careful planning. The collaboration among group members must also withstand the multiple trials necessary for the data to be reliable. The data must be recorded according to protocol each and every time.

The development of scientific research skills also involves the interpretation and representation of data. Analyzing the data at the middle school level will not involve tests of statistical significance, but rather percentages and averages.

Creative thinking needs to be encouraged and fostered. By developing the critical thinking skills needed in science, students will learn to tolerate varying degrees of collaboration, uncertainty, and risk-taking, all of which are inherent in the practice of science.

PRIOR KNOWLEDGE

Students should have carried out several experiments and investigations. Guide the class project so that it is feasible and relevant to content.

INSTRUCTIONAL SEQUENCE

1. Select several possible research projects for students to complete in a designated time period. These projects should be science-based and require students to collaborate. Some possible projects include the following:
   - What is the best place to plant a garden to attract bees on school grounds? Research the problems facing pollinating insects, such as bees, and find the best type of plants for the garden. How might the garden be maintained?
   - How can alternative energy sources, such as wind turbines and solar panels, be used to power something at school, such as a weather station? Research the need for renewable energy sources and design a way to use the energy source to power a hot water heater or a weather station.
   - How could rainwater be captured from the school roof and used to irrigate a vegetable garden? Research how to engineer an irrigation system so that the rainwater easily flows where needed.

   In addition, there are many types of community projects, such as wetland restoration and community gardens, that students can join. Local environmental organizations or the public library may have projects listed on their websites. Students can then research the function of native wetland plants, for instance, and how these plants help maintain wetlands by preventing erosion and filtering out pollutants.

2. Once the class has decided on a project, students can work together in groups of 3–4 to complete Lesson 5.3 Team Research Project. The responses from these handouts and ensuing classroom discussions will serve as the springboard for the planning of the project. The logistics of the class project will have to be outlined, and responsibilities for each student must be delegated. See Figure 6 for sample responses to Lesson 5.3 Team Research Project.

What are some ideas for our project?	*We will plant a buffer garden between the parking lot and the lake.*
How is our project related to science? What area of science relates best to our project?	*Native wetland plants filter out pollutants. When it rains, dangerous substances like oil and gas can be carried to the lake. The area of science related to this project is environmental science.*
What kind of background research do we need to do?	*We need to research how plants filter out pollutants. We also need to research which plants would be best for our garden.*
What kinds of material do we need?	*We will need gardening tools, potting soil, native wetland plants, and water quality measurement tools.*
How much time do we have for our project?	*2 months*
What are the responsibilities of each group member?	*The responsibilities of each group member will be researching, planting, and monitoring the buffer garden. We will also monitor the lake to see if the garden helps improve the water quality.*
What will the final project look like?	*We will have a garden of native wetland plants between the lake and the parking lot. We should also have better water quality in the lake.*
Does our project need to be maintained after we leave the school? If so, how will we maintain it?	*No, it does not.*
Do we have the approval of the teacher and principal?	*We will ask for approval before beginning.*

Figure 6. Sample responses for Lesson 5.3 Team Research Project.

3. Continue outlining the project and procedure with students. Projects will vary depending on school and class needs. As an example, consider the experiment my students conducted at Lake Taylor Middle School several years ago (outlined in Figure 6). We tested the water quality of the lake next to the school to see if the water quality was better or worse next to the school parking lot. When we looked at the data, we saw the water quality was worse next to the parking lot. We planned a buffer garden with

the horticulture students at the nearby vocational school. Some students researched native plants that would be ideal for this garden, while others investigated how plants can filter out pollutants.

4. Have students gather and analyze data. Because this project involves a team of student researchers, the data may be too cumbersome to analyze with calculators. Microsoft Excel makes it easy for students to record, analyze, and represent data visually. There are easy-to-follow tutorials as well as YouTube videos for students to gain proficiency with this software. In the case of the aforementioned example, we gathered water-quality data (pH, dissolved oxygen, nitrogen levels, and turbidity readings) before, during, and after the garden was planted.

5. The next step in the research project is to draw conclusions. If the data are accurate and valid, students can draw conclusions based on the data. Once again, strong data come from careful planning.

6. Once students draw conclusions, ask them to write a reflection in their science notebooks: *What went well in the research project? What needs modification in the future?* Discuss responses with the class.

EXTENSION ACTIVITY

Invite experts from your community, such as science faculty from local universities or scientists from other organizations, to visit. Have students present their research project to these experts, who can ask questions about students' presentations. In this way, potential future collaboration with scientist mentors can be forged.

ASSESSMENT OBSERVATIONS

*   Students should be actively engaged in the research project during each step. Ask formative questions throughout the process to gauge student engagement (e.g., "Why is it important for us to always follow the same procedure to get data?").
*   Students should collaborate with their groups.

LESSON 5.3

Team Research Project

Directions: Fill out this handout with your team's ideas about the project your class will research and carry out.

What are some ideas for our project?	
How is our project related to science? What area of science relates best to our project?	
What kind of background research do we need to do?	
What kinds of materials do we need?	

Team Research Project, continued

How much time do we have for our project?	
What are the responsibilities of each group member?	
What will the final project look like?	
Does our project need to be maintained after we leave the school? If so, how will we maintain it?	
Do we have the approval of the teacher and principal?	

POSTASSESSMENT

Students act as scientists when they observe, make inferences, formulate research questions, and conduct experiments. Data literacy (i.e., interpreting and communicating data using visual representations) is developed through practice and taking apart the components of graphs, as discussed in Unit 3. The research that students and scientists carry out is built on prior science research. Students are active participants in the scientific process when they engage in research and experimentation, thereby adding to scientific knowledge. When students present their research to others in the class, they can respond to questions about their investigations so that they can more clearly evaluate the components of their experimental design. Practice in this process and the feedback from their peers and teachers will help students hone their science skills.

This postassessment can be used at the end of Unit 3 or at the end of the school year. To make this an open-ended postassessment, you may take away the answer choices. The last section asks students to build upon and fine-tune the experiment. Possible modifications to the experiment include: conduct multiple trials, vary the amounts of CO_2, and measure the amounts with a CO_2 sensor.

POSTASSESSMENT

Directions: Consider the scenario and answer the questions that follow.

Sam conducted a science experiment in which he modeled the greenhouse effect and global warming. He set up three large glass jars outside on the grass in the sun. Jar A had no lid, Jar B had a lid, and Jar C had extra carbon dioxide added (from a CO_2 bike tire cartridge) and a lid. All jars had the same thermometers placed inside. Every 5 minutes, Sam recorded the temperatures of the jars. He did this for one hour and recorded the following results.

Average Temperature of Jar A	Average Temperature of Jar B	Average Temperature of Jar C
88° F	97° F	120° F

1. What is the purpose of the CO_2 levels in Sam's experiment?
   a. It is the control.
   b. It is the dependent variable.
   c. It is the independent variable.
   d. It is a constant.

2. How did Sam use the location of his experiment?
   a. It is the control.
   b. It is the dependent variable.
   c. It is the independent variable.
   d. It is a constant.

3. What is the role of the temperature in his experiment?
   a. It is the control.
   b. It is the dependent variable.
   c. It is the independent variable.
   d. It is a constant.

4. Which statement would serve as a hypothesis for this experiment?
   a. Changing the CO_2 levels will affect the temperatures inside the jars.
   b. Jars placed outside will heat up faster than ones inside.
   c. If I change the temperature, the CO_2 levels will be affected.
   d. If I use plastic jars, the temperatures will be affected.

Postassessment, continued

5. What conclusions do the results of Sam's experiment support?
   a. Placing jars in the sun will increase the heat inside them.

   b. Temperatures from glass and plastic jars differ greatly.

   c. Sam can draw no conclusions from his results.

   d. Adding CO_2 to the air inside the jars will increase temperatures.

Extend Your Thinking

Now it's your turn! Using Sam's results as preliminary research, you are going to build upon his experiment. Please write a paragraph about how you could fine-tune this experiment so that you can draw strong conclusions from your data.

ANSWER KEY

PREASSESSMENT

1. c
2. d
3. a
4. b
5. a
6. c
7. b
8. b
9. b
10. d

LESSON 2.2 EVALUATING HYPOTHESES

Hypothesis	Is This Hypothesis Testable and Unbiased?	Revised Hypothesis
If I change the amount of salt in the recipe, the soup will taste bad.	No	Answers will vary. Sample answer: If I change the amount of salt in the recipe, its taste will change according to the ratings of the tasters.

Hypothesis	Is This Hypothesis Testable and Unbiased?	Revised Hypothesis
Blue jays prefer sunflower seeds to thistle seeds.	No	Answers will vary. Sample answer: Blue jays will show a seed preference if given a choice of sunflower seeds and thistle seeds.
The growth of plants is affected by the amount of light they receive.	Yes	Acceptable as is.
If I change the air pressure outside of the balloon, the pressure inside the balloon increases.	No	Answers will vary. Sample answer: If I change the air pressure outside the balloon, the pressure inside the balloon will be affected.

LESSON 2.3 EVALUATING VARIABLES

Data	Discrete or Continuous?	Reasoning
The density of a liquid as it is heated	Continuous	Answers will vary.
The number of students who use cell phones to complete classroom assignments	Discrete	Answers will vary.
The volume of a liquid before and after it is frozen	Continuous	Answers will vary.
The number of "heads" each time a coin is flipped	Discrete	Answers will vary.
The average monthly temperature in a location throughout the year	Continuous	Answers will vary.

LESSON 2.4 CHOOSING GRAPH TYPES

Answers will vary. Possible answers include the following.

Research Question	Type of Graph	Justification
How does the amount of sea ice in the Arctic change throughout the year?	Line graph	The amount of sea ice is measured over a period of time.
What proportion of recyclable waste is thrown away at our school?	Pie chart	I am looking at a proportion of waste out of the total (100%) waste.
How did the average winter temperature for last year compare to the average winter temperature for this year?	Bar graph	I am comparing the average temperature this year with the temperature for last year.
What are the ages of students in our class?	Histogram	There is variability in our ages.

LESSON 3.3 UNCOVERING MISCONCEPTIONS

Claim	Misconception or Fact?	Evidence
The sky is blue because it reflects the ocean.	Misconception	Blue wavelengths are shorter and scatter faster than other wavelengths on the visible spectrum of light. That is why we see the sky as blue.
Your body's blood is blue before it reaches your lungs.	Misconception	Blood is always red!
Air has mass.	Fact	When you inflate a balloon, you are increasing the mass inside the balloon.

Claim	Misconception or Fact?	Evidence
Seasons are the result of Earth's tilt and Earth's varying distance in its elliptical orbit around the sun.	*Misconception*	*Seasons are the result of Earth's tilt. Earth varies in its distance from the sun in its elliptical orbit. Earth is closer to the sun in its orbit in January (perihelion) and farther from the sun in July (aphelion). The tilt causes the seasons, not Earth's distance differences in its elliptical orbit.*
Our atmosphere is 100% oxygen.	*Misconception*	*Earth's atmosphere is 78% nitrogen, 21% oxygen, 0.9% argon, and 0.1% trace elements.*
Most earthquakes happen near plate boundaries.	*Fact*	*Earthquakes tend to occur on plate boundaries, such as the Ring of Fire.*

LESSON 4.3 KWL EARTH MOTIONS

What do you think you know about Earth's position and motions?	What do you want to learn about Earth's position and motions?	What have you learned about Earth's position and motions?
Rotation	*How does this cause day and night?*	*Answers will vary.*
Revolution	*How long is Earth's orbit?* *How does it compare to that of other planets?* *What is the effect of Earth's tilt?*	*Answers will vary.*
Third planet from the sun	*Why is Earth the only planet to have life (as we know it)?* *Why is Earth the only planet with liquid water?* *What is the importance of Earth's tilt?*	*Answers will vary.*

LESSON 5.1 EXPERIMENTAL DESIGN

Independent Variable	*Black or white lining in the solar oven*
Dependent Variable	*The temperature reached after 45 minutes (or another specified time)*
Constants	*Same solar oven construction; boxes face the same direction and are exposed to the same temperature*
Control Group	*Solar oven with no lining*
Hypothesis	*The temperature reached by the solar ovens after 45 minutes will be affected by the color of the lining inside the box. (The color of the lining will affect the temperature inside the oven.)*
Materials	*Pizza box, foil, plastic wrap, tape, black or white paper, s'mores*
Procedure	*See Lesson 5.1 Instructional Sequence.*
Data	*Temperatures recorded during and after the experiment.*
Analysis	*Answers will vary.*
Conclusion	*The color of the lining affected the temperature inside the boxes. The boxes with black paper reached hotter temperatures than the white or unlined boxes.*
Future Experiments	*Answers will vary.*

POSTASSESSMENT

1. c
2. a
3. b
4. a
5. d

Extend Your Thinking

Sample answer: *In order to model the greenhouse effect and global warming, I will set up nine large transparent glass empty jars. Jars in Group A will have no lid, Jars in Group B will have lids, and Jars in Group C will have extra carbon dioxide added (from a CO_2 bike tire cartridge) and a lid. All jars will have the same thermometers placed inside and be put outside on the grass in the sun. I will record the temperature in the jars every 5 minutes for one hour and then analyze the results.*

REFERENCES

Biological Sciences Curriculum Studies. (2012). *I can use the Identify and Interpret (I²) Strategy.* Retrieved from https://media.bscs.org/icans/Icans_I2_SE.pdf

Chambers, D. W. (1983). Stereotypic images of the scientist: The draw-a-scientist test. *Science Education, 6,* 255–265. https://doi.org/10.1002/sce.3730670213

Choi, J. (2004). *"The nature of science": An activity for the first day of class.* Retrieved from http://www.scienceteacherprogram.org/genscience/Choi04.html

Webber, H., Nelson, S. J., Weatherbee, R., Zoellick, B., & Schauffler, M. (2014). The graph choice chart. *Science Teacher, 81*(8), 37–43.

ABOUT THE AUTHOR

Lenore Teevan teaches Earth science and AP Biology at Booker T. Washington High School in Norfolk, VA. For the past 14 years, she has taught science to students near the unique Chesapeake Bay ecosystem. She hopes to inspire her students through her teaching and summer experiences as a PolarTREC teacher and a National Oceanic and Atmospheric Administration (NOAA) Teacher at Sea.

NEXT GENERATION SCIENCE STANDARDS ALIGNMENT

Unit/Lesson	Next Generation Science Standards
Unit 2	5-ESS1-1. Support an argument that differences in the apparent brightness of the sun compared to other stars is due to their relative distances from Earth. 5-ESS1-2. Represent data in graphical displays to reveal patterns of daily changes in length and direction of shadows, day and night, and the seasonal appearance of some stars in the night sky.
Unit 4	5-ESS3-1. Obtain and combine information about ways individual communities use science ideas to protect the Earth's resources and environment.
Unit 5	3-5-ETS1-1. Define a simple design problem reflecting a need or a want that includes specified criteria for success and constraints on materials, time, or cost. 3-5-ETS1-2. Generate and compare multiple possible solutions to a problem based on how well each is likely to meet the criteria and constraints of the problem. 3-5-ETS1-3. Plan and carry out fair tests in which variables are controlled and failure points are considered to identify aspects of a model or prototype that can be improved. 5-ESS2-1. Develop a model using an example to describe ways the geosphere, biosphere, hydrosphere, and/or atmosphere interact. 5-ESS2-2. Describe and graph the amounts and percentages of water and fresh water in various reservoirs to provide evidence about the distribution of water on Earth. MS-ETS1-1. Define the criteria and constraints of a design problem with sufficient precision to ensure a successful solution, taking into account relevant scientific principles and potential impacts on people and the natural environment that may limit possible solutions. MS-ETS1-2. Evaluate competing design solutions using a systematic process to determine how well they meet the criteria and constraints of the problem.

Unit/Lesson	Next Generation Science Standards
Unit 5, continued	MS-ETS1-3. Analyze data from tests to determine similarities and differences among several design solutions to identify the best characteristics of each that can be combined into a new solution to better meet the criteria for success. MS-ETS1-4. Develop a model to generate data for iterative testing and modification of a proposed object, tool, or process such that an optimal design can be achieved.